The Tears of Lady Meng

The Tears of Lady Meng

A parable of people's political theology

C. S. Song

ORBIS BOOKS
Maryknoll, New York 10545

The Catholic Foreign Mission Society of America (Maryknoll) recruits and trains people for overseas missionary service. Through Orbis Books Maryknoll aims to foster the international dialogue that is essential to mission. The books published, however, reflect the opinions of their authors and are not meant to represent the official position of the society.

First published as No. 11 in the World Council of Churches Risk book series, Copyright © 1981 by World Council of Churches, 150, route de Ferney, 1211, Geneva 20 Switzerland

U.S. edition 1982 by Orbis Books, Maryknoll, NY 10545

Typeset in Switzerland and printed and bound in the United States of America

Library of Congress Cataloging in Publication Data

Song, Choan-Seng, 1929-
    The tears of Lady Meng.

    "Expanded version of a D.T. Niles memorial
lecture, entitled 'Political theology of living
in Christ with people,' given at the General
Assembly of the Christian Conference of Asia
held in Bangalore, India, May 18-28, 1981"—Pref.
    1. Christianity and politics—Addresses,
essays, lectures. I. Title.
BR115.P7S615   1982   261.7   82-2295
ISBN 0-88344-505-0 (pbk.)   AACR2

Preface

This is an expanded version of a D.T. Niles Memorial Lecture, entitled "Political Theology of Living in Christ with People", given at the General Assembly of the Christian Conference of Asia held in Bangalore, India, May 18-28, 1981. What could be more appropriate, then, than to repeat here the introductory remarks I made before giving the lecture, in place of a preface for this version? This is what I said:

It is really good to be here! Faces are familiar and friendly. Voices are strong and confident. Colours are gay and bold. What I feel in this hall, in this Assembly and in this city is the pulse of life — life seeking to encounter meaning, liberation and destiny. I am grateful to Dr Yap Kim Hao, general secretary of the Christian Conference of Asia, and his colleagues who have extended to me the invitation to give one of the D.T. Niles Memorial Lectures. I consider this a great personal honour.

I must confess, however, at the outset, that I am not one of those who can claim the privilege of having had close association with D.T. Niles (1908-1970). The closest I got to him were the few fleeting moments in which we shared an elevator ride at Hotel Fortuna in Hong Kong in 1966 during the first Asian Faith and Order Conference on "Confessing the Faith in Asia Today." He was absorbed in discussing Conference matters with his old colleagues. As a young, inexperienced theologian, I watched him with some shyness and with a sense of wonder. It was the only occasion I saw D.T. Niles at close range. And I must say he was an impressive figure seen at close quarters as well as from a distance.

When I received the invitation to give a Niles memorial lecture, that short elevator ride came back to my mind. I then took a crash course on the life and theology of D.T. Niles and read as much as I could lay my hand on at the library of the Ecumenical Centre in Geneva. There was much that I learnt about him and from him. What particularly impressed me was his struggle within the captivity of dialectical theology as an Asian preacher, evangelist and pioneer theologian. He had to live and wrestle with many theological contradictions. His agony over those contradictions must have reached a climax at that Conference on *Confessing the Faith in Asia Today* in 1966.

I consider that Conference to be a landmark in the history of the churches in Asia. Into it the past flowed, and out of it the new struggled to be born. D.T. Niles, who had shaped the form and thought of East Asia Christian Conference, now called Christian Conference of Asia, since its inception up to that point, must have felt tremendous birthpangs in his theological being. As far as I can judge, he was not able to shake off the spell cast on him by dialectical theology. But his agony, created by the contradictions of having to live in that captivity in the midst of cultures, histories and religions outside the Judaeo-Christian traditions, developed into a creative force, bringing into being theological actions and reflections we experience in Asia today. From "Confessing the Faith in Asia Today" in 1966 to "Living in Christ with People" in 1981 has been an agonizing and eventful journey. And if D.T. Niles were here with us today, he would have been, I am sure, a most prominent Asian theologian who had left behind him the captivity of traditional theology to embrace whole-heartedly the theology of Living in Christ with People.

Our best tribute to D.T. Niles therefore is to pick up where he left off, and to press forward in our theological vocation in Asia today and tomorrow.

Now to my lecture this morning. Its background was already set yesterday by the communication from Seoul, regarding renewed political repression, read to us during the worship service, and also by the presentation of our sisters portraying the oppression they have suffered in the male-dominated society in Asia. Not always through their own choice Christians and churches in Asia are becoming more and more drawn into social and political issues and problems. One of many urgent questions asked by many of us today is: What is our political theology? My lecture this morning reflects my own personal thinking on the question. It is *per-*

sonal, I must emphasize. But being part of Taiwan and of Asia by birth and, I hope, also by right, I may strike a chord in the hearts of some of you in this Assembly Hall.

My prologue is already getting a little too long. But just one more word. Besides reflecting on a possible political theology in Asian settings, I hope I can show that theology is a *synthetic* art, as it were, projecting a picture, an image, a symbol, about reality on the basis of the Bible *and* out of the life that flows in our veins and in the veins of our people. *The Story of God* — this is what theology essentially is — is the story of people, not just of Jewish-Christian people, but of millions and tens of millions of people here in Asia.

It remains for me to thank Claudius Ceccon, a Brazilian artist, who puts his artistic talent and imagination at the service of the Christian faith and theology. His drawings in this booklet speak more profoundly than mere words can convey. I also owe a word of thanks to Marlin van Elderen, editor of *Risk Books*, and Jan Kok, publications manager, of the World Council of Churches.

This happened in the reign of the wicked, unjust Emperor Ch'in Shih Huang-ti. He was afraid at this time that the Huns would break into the country from the north and not leave him any peace.

In order to keep them in check, he decided to build a wall along the whole northern frontier of China. But no sooner was one piece built than another fell down, and the wall made no progress.

Then a wise (!) man said to him: "A wall like this, which is over ten thousand miles long, can be built only if you immure a human being in every mile of the wall. Each mile will then have its guardian." It was easy for the Emperor to follow this advice, for he regarded his subjects as so much grass and weeds, and the whole land began to tremble under this threat.

Plans were then made for human sacrifice in great numbers. At the last minute "an ingenious scholar" suggested to the Emperor that it would be sufficient to sacrifice a man called Wan "since Wan means ten thousand". Soldiers were dispatched at once to seize Wan who was sitting with his bride at the wedding feast. He was carried off by the heartless soldiers, leaving Lady Meng, his bride, in tears.

There was nothing to be done, and she sat down and wept.

Her weeping so affected the wall that it collapsed and laid bare her husband's bones.

When the Emperor heard of Meng Chiang and how she was seeking her husband, he wanted to see her himself. When she was brought before him, her unearthly beauty so struck him that he decided to make her Empress. She knew she could not avoid her fate, and therefore she agreed on three conditions.

First, a festival lasting forty-nine days should be held in honour of her husband; second, the Emperor, with all his officials, should be present at the burial; and third, he should build a terrace forty-nine feet high on the bank of the river, where she wanted to make a sacrifice to her husband. ... Ch'in Shih Huang-ti granted all her requests at once.

When everything was ready she climbed on to the terrace
and began to curse the Emperor in a loud voice for all his
cruelty and wickedness. Although this made the Emperor
very angry, he held his peace.

But when she jumped from the terrace into the river, he flew
into a rage and ordered his soldiers to cut up her body into
little pieces and grind her bones to powder.

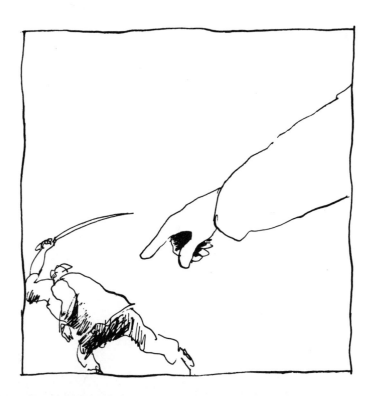

When they did this, the little pieces changed into little silver fish, in which the soul of faithful Meng Chiang lives for ever.

The Wall every Stone of which cost a human Life

The Great Wall is one of the marvels of China, even of the world. Winding through North China from Shanhaikuan on the coast into Kansu Province in the Northwest, it stretches for more than 1,500 miles in space and for more than two thousand years in time. In recent years it has been transformed from historic ruins into a cultural glory. It is visited by Presidents of powerful nations. It has served as a stage for geo-political games played with great relish by aggressive politicians. It has also won admiration from innocent tourists from both near and far. The Great Wall, or the Ten Thousand Li Long Wall as the Chinese call it, has leapt out of the past to play a new role in the life of individuals, nations, and the world.

But do Presidents of powerful nations know? Are those who play "body-politics" aware? Can tens of thousands of tourists imagine? Will the world care to be reminded? It is said that a million people perished in building the Wall, that every stone cost a human life. Small wonder, Shih Huang-ti, the despotic emperor of the first empire of China in the third century B.C., has won undying hatred for building this defence wall against the nomads of the Mongolian steppe.

Over the centuries there have grown around this monument of cruelty stories and legends depicting the endless tragedies that invaded the lives of common people, humiliating them, uprooting them, and destroying them. Reflected in these stories of the people — folk stories — is not only the remote past, but the immediate present and perhaps the distant future. Projected in them is the universal struggle of people to be human, free, and authentic.

I would like to tell you one of those folktales as we wrestle together with the political ethic of the cross of Jesus. It is a folktale called "The Faithful Lady Meng".

This happened in the reign of the wicked, unjust Emperor Ch'in Shih Huang-ti. He was afraid at this time that the Huns would break into the country from the north and not leave him any peace. In order to keep them in check, he decided to build a wall along the whole northern frontier of China. But no sooner was one piece built than another fell down, and the wall made no progress. Then a wise (!) man said to him: "A wall like this, which is over ten thousand miles long, can be built only if you immure a human being in every mile of the wall. Each mile will then have its guardian." It was easy for the emperor to follow this advice, for he regarded his subjects as so much grass and weeds, and the whole land began to tremble under this threat.

Plans were then made for human sacrifice in great numbers. At the last minute "an ingenious scholar" suggested to the Emperor that it would be sufficient to sacrifice a man called Wan "since Wan means ten thousand". Soldiers were dispatched at once to seize Wan who was sitting with his bride at the wedding feast. He was carried off by the heartless soldiers, leaving Lady Meng, his bride, in tears.

Eventually, heedless of the fatigues of the journey, she travelled over mountains and through rivers to find the bones of her husband. When she saw the stupendous wall she did not know how to find the bones. There was nothing to be done, and she sat down and wept. Her weeping so affected the wall that it collapsed and laid bare her husband's bones.

When the Emperor heard of Meng Chiang and how she was seeking her husband, he wanted to see her himself. When she was brought before him, her unearthly beauty so struck him that he decided to make her Empress. She knew she could not avoid her fate, and therefore she agreed on three conditions. First, a festival lasting forty-nine days should be held in honour of her husband; second, the Emperor, with all his officials, should be present at the burial; and third, he should build a terrace forty-nine feet high on the bank of the river, where she wanted to make a sacrifice to her husband. ... Ch'in Shih Huang-ti granted all her requests at once.

When everything was ready she climbed on to the terrace and began to curse the Emperor in a loud voice for all his cruelty and wickedness. Although this made the Emperor very angry, he held his peace. But when she jumped from the terrace into the river, he flew into a rage and ordered his soldiers to cut up her body into little pieces and grind her bones to powder. When they did this, the little pieces changed into little silver fish, in which the soul of the faithful Meng Chiang lives for ever.[1]

The Wall made no Progress

It is very strange, isn't it ? The wall that would defend the nation from nomadic invaders made no progress. "No sooner was one piece built", the folktale tells us, "than another fell down." Was there something wrong with the architectural blueprints? This could not have been the case. The officials in charge of this colossal work must have hired all the first-class architects available at that time for even today the Great Wall is considered a remarkable engineering feat. Perhaps the materials used were of inferior quality and could not stand up to the demands called for in the plans? This too must be ruled out, because at stake was imperial defence. In actual fact bricks and stones in the Wall are found bound together by excellent mortar. Many of the stones are huge blocks hewn from granite, some of them fourteen feet long and three or four feet thick![2]

If it was not due to faulty plans or material of poor quality, then the little progress in the construction of the Wall must have been the result of sabotage by the workers. But again this is absolutely out of the question. How could the conscript labourers under strict oversight of the imperial army out-manoeuvre the emperor's order?

Still, the Wall made no progress — the Wall essential for national defence. Even we are puzzled. We want to know

why. Like our ancient forebears in China, and for that matter in Egypt, Babylonia, even in Israel and Judah, we are very defence-conscious. We want to defend our national honour; this is patriotism. We are in duty bound to fight for our land; this is good citizenship. We must protect the truth of our faith and our religion; this is "orthodoxism". We defend our nation, our religion, our cause, right to left. We behave, as individuals and as a collective body, as if our life and our survival depend totally on how strong our defence-instincts are, how effectively our security mechanism works. Surely it is a cause for alarm that the emperor's great wall made no progress. Even when our own little defence walls do not get a good start we have reason enough to panic.

Meanwhile, the whole tragic affair of the Wall is slowly unfolded in the folktale. In the midst of great agitation, the emperor's counsellor offered the following counsel: "A wall like this, which is over ten thousand miles long, can be built only if you immure a human being in every mile of the wall. Each mile then will have its guardian." What a counsel! Ten thousand lives for building the Wall! This is insanity! This is inhumanity! But the emperor responded to the counsel as if it were a flash of revelation from heaven. And the folk story-teller shares with us a terrible secret: "The emperor regarded his subjects as so much grass and weeds."

This is the starting point of the political theology embedded in this folktale. Do folktales contain theological and political insights? Yes, folktales too have a political theology. In fact, the kind of political theology we find in folktales can be more genuine, more powerful, more heartbreaking and also more heartening than many "Christian" political theologies. Folktale political theology is conceived in the womb of people's experience. In the darkness of that womb a new life is hatched in people's tears and laughter; it struggles to grow in people's hope and despair. When the time comes, it bursts open the depths of humanity and becomes part of the world of joy and pain. "The history of humankind," says an American sociologist, "is a history of pain."[3]

How true! But it is only half the truth. "The history of humankind," we must go on to say, "is the history of hope."

Pain alone does not bring sense to life. Pain alone does not reveal the meaning of history. Pain alone does not ennoble humanity. And pain alone does not make the present worth living. There must be, besides pain, hope. There must be, besides the present, a future. There must be, besides one dreadful destruction after another, one joyful construction after another. Life is a race against pain. History is a never-ending process of construction on the ruins of destruction. It is this kind of political theology that we find in some of the finest folk literature, folk songs, folk dance, and folk dramas. This is the politcal theology of the people, or the *minjung*, as Korean Christians like to call it. In these "folk-things", we Christians may perceive reflections of the cross.

In them we may also gain a glimpse of the resurrection. This will surprise us, humble us, and excite us. After all, "Christian" political theology should be no more and no less than "folk" political theology — political theology of the people. This in fact was the political theology of Jesus Christ — the theology of living with people.

Emperors and rulers too have their political theology. This we must know. This people must be fully aware of. The essence of political theology held by those who monopolize political and military powers is what we have in our folktale: "The Emperor regarded his subjects as so much grass and weeds." This was the premise of Shih Huang-ti's political theology. This was the assumption of the Pharaohs' political theology — the Pharaohs who wasted and destroyed millions and tens of millions of human lives in the building of pyramids in order to manifest royal glory and to achieve the vain hope of physical immortality. This, too, was the justification of Hitler's demonic political theology which drove several millions of Jews to death in the gas chambers. The atrocious genocide committed by the Khmer Rouge of Pol Pot's Cambodia is still too painful to mention; here too people were treated as "so much grass and weeds".

But we have not finished our listing. The same premise, the same assumption and the same justification underlies the national policy of many repressive regimes in Asia today. All of these regimes, says a speaker at the consultation on "Patterns of Domination and People's Movements in Asia", organized by the Christian Conference of Asia and held in Manila, Philippines, in 1979,

> stress the moral claims of the state: national discipline, national unity, the importance of national development and the mischievousness and divisiveness of politics.[4]

The rulers who regard people as so much grass and weeds, the power-holders who use people as mere tools for economic development and national defence, make moral claims too. Their moral claims are said to be guided by the policy of the highest order — national security.

A God called National Security

What is national security? What does it look like? What shape does it have? It is a god — a cruel, savage god! It is a god that feeds on human flesh and blood. Since ancient times, the world has known many many gods with very large appetites for human flesh. Practically every tribe and every nation, East or West, had that kind of god. Animal flesh was not good enough for them. They refused to be placated with animal blood. To gain their favour, nothing less than human blood would do. The ancient Phoenicians offered human babies on a red-hot altar to their fire god Moloch. The Canaanites had to cater to the unnatural lust of Chemosh with human victims. At the Saiva temple at Tanjore in India, until two hundred years ago a male child was sacrificed every Friday evening at a shrine of Kali. The ancient Romans are said to have put corn-thieves to death as a sacrifice to Ceres. In Israel and Judah, at times, those "dedicated" to Yahweh by a solemn vow were put to death.[5]

In comparison with these bloody gods, many deities worshipped by people in many pantheons seem quite tame and harmless. They are impotent gods. You could gibe at them as well as worship them:

> For the carved images of the nations are a sham,
> they are nothing but timber cut from the forest,
> worked with his chisel by a craftsman;
> he adorns it with silver and gold,
> fastening them on with hammer and nails
> so that they do not fall apart.
> They can no more speak than a scarecrow in a plot of cucumbers;
> they must be carried, for they cannot walk.
> Do not be afraid of them: they can do no harm,
> and they have no power to do good (Jer. 10:3-5).

For all we know, Jeremiah got away unharmed with such disrespect he had shown towards gods and idols. But he was not so lucky and nearly paid with his life for advocating surrender to the invading Babylonian armies as the only way to national salvation. Many of the gods and idols Jeremiah

ridiculed have disappeared. But this savage god — national
security — not only has not disappeared but has become
more savage. In the name of national security political opposition is condemned as sedition, and brutally suppressed.
No one can offend this god and get away free. The taboo
surrounding this idol is hard to break by democratic
movements. Democratic movements — movements of the
people — are most offensive to the cult of national security.
They upset internal stability, and invite the danger of inva-
sion by external enemies. That is why we have seen this god
of national security raging in great fury in many Asian
capitals in recent years. Charges are fabricated against
political dissidents. False confessions are extracted from
human rights fighters under torture. The military court is
then duly summoned to pronounce the pre-determined verdict on the victims. These martial law court trials are ritual
murders committed on the altar of national security, the
supreme god. Such ritual murders committed as a matter of
routine to defend the cult of national security have obscured
ideological boundaries among Asian nations. If they take
place in a capitalist capital, they also take place in a socialist
capital. If they are staged in a "free and democratic" nation, so are they performed in an "unfree and autocratic"
nation. A strange convergence has occurred in Asia today
— a convergence of ideologically antagonistic regimes
before the altar of the deity whose name is national
security.The pretexts may be different — commitment to
historical materialism, recovery of lost territory, reunifica-
tion of a divided nation .... But it comes down to one and
the same thing: absolute dedication to national security.

But people are not deceived. Even our folk story-teller in
ancient China was not duped. In reality, it is the question of
power. The emperor who was able to carry out the murder
of ten thousand lives to build a defence wall must have been
a powerful emperor. The ruling political party which is able
to mobilize police, military and judicial forces to arrest, try
and imprison opposition politicians must be a formidable
party. Idolatry of national security is the idolatry of power.
Among the African peoples it has been observed that "the
more powerful the nation, the grander the (human)

sacrifice."[6] The immensity of human sacrifice becomes the measure of the power held by the ruler. That is why a repressive regime controls people's minds with force. It responds to the voice of opposition with intimidation. And it reacts to open protest with military power.

Here the true nature of the cult of national security is uncovered. The cult secures *not* the security of the nation *but* the security of the ruling party. The cult enhances *not* the security of the people *but* the security of the autocratic ruler. Our folktale says with unerring insight: "The Emperor regarded his subjects as so much grass and weeds." People are disposable as grass while the ruler is not. The security of people is dispensable whereas the security of the power-holder is not. This cult of power is more frightening than the cult of Moloch or Chemosh. It can reduce human beings to mere grass and weeds.

This savage god of national security and power is a greedy god. Insatiable greed is another horrible characterisitc of this god. It devoured one million human beings in the construction of the Great Wall. The frightful fact is that the more it devours, the greedier it becomes. It demands more and more human sacrifice. It lusts after more and more human flesh. It thirsts for more and more human blood. This, for example, is the god of the frantic arms race — one of the manifestations of this greedy god in our world and in our time. The race for armaments is a race for national security, so people are told. But it contributes, in fact, to the concentration of power in the hands of the already powerful ruler. The result, as affirmed by the Vatican, is "the obvious contradiction between the waste involved in the overproduction of military devices and the extent of unsatisfied vital needs." The contradiction

> is in itself an act of aggression against those who are the victims of it. It is an act of aggression which amounts to a crime, for even when armaments are not used, by their cost alone, they kill the poor by causing them to starve.[7]

It is no longer a matter of one million lives. It is a matter of one billion lives, and even more. A policy made ostensibly to enhance national security, even if it may cost one billion lives, is considered moral. A strategy designed to promote national defence, even if it devours more than one-third of the gross national product, which is the case in most Third World countries, is deemed justifiable.

The Soviet Union has long succumbed to the tyranny of this insatiable god. No outsider to the Soviet State secrets could know how many roubles she burns on the altar of this god. But the sad fact is that even the United States, a nation that claims to abhor idolatry, increasingly submits herself to the perverse charm of this god of destruction. Her present administration has proposed to cut by one-third her 8 million dollar foreign aid programme, which represents less than a third of one per cent of the 2.6 trillion U.S. gross national product. In the midst of all the talk of mercilessly axing the budgets, military spending not only escapes the cuts but will get substantial increase. In his first address to the Congress on February 18, 1981, President Reagan said that his administration plans to ask Congress for an extra $1.3 billion for military spending in the current fiscal year of 1981, $7.2 billion more in 1982, $20.7 billion in 1983, $27 billion in 1984. In 1985 there will be an additional asking of $50.2 billion and in 1986, $63.1 billion![8] Who could comprehend such staggering figures? On top of all this, human rights will no longer be a high priority in American foreign policy. In dismay we cannot help asking: Who is going to suffer because of all this? The answer is clear. This, says a newspaper editorial, "would be a sharp, indiscriminate blow to the world's poor"[9], and to those who struggle for the basic human rights of freedom, justice and democracy in the Third World. Under the reign of this greedy god, the poor and the oppresed have little hope of "raising their heads above the sky" (ch'ut t'au t'n) as people in Taiwan say.

Plea with Tears

This powerful, savage and greedy god worshipped by emperors, presidents and generals! This idolatry of power before which people tremble in fear! What kind of political theology would be a match for it? What sort of power ethic would be powerful enough to cope with it? Many of us in

Asia ask such questions, particularly those of us who have
seen and experienced the tragedy of the Kwangju uprising in
Korea in May 1980, the suppression of the Human Rights
Day Rally in Taiwan in 1979, the suspension of the writ of
habeas corpus — the right of prisoners to challenge their
detention — under martial law rule in the Philippines,
military presence at every level of government and big
business in Indonesia. Buddhists, too, asked these questions
through self-immolation at the height of the Vietnam War.
The writers who contributed to the erection of the
Democracy Wall in Peking also searched for answers to
these basic questions. These are people's questions — Buddhists or Christians, Hindus or Muslims, believers or non-
believers. This is the quest for a people's political theology
as against the rulers' political theology. This is the birth-
pang of a people's power ethic to overcome the dictators'
power ethic. To put it in the language of Christian faith,
here is the search for a political theology and power ethic
of living in Christ with people.

As far as Lady Meng is concerned, she knows what she
should do. Her husband was taken from her and buried in
the Great Wall. The Wall has been completed, but her duty
towards her murdered husband has not yet been completed.

She must bring back his bones and bury them where he belongs — his ancestral home. It was a long and dangerous journey which she had to make from her home to the Great Wall. Finally she reached the Wall — the Wall that took her husband's life, broke up her family and deprived her of the joy and hope that the union of husband and wife alone could give. But at once she realized that she was confronted with a humanly impossible task. The Wall stared at her with cold arrogance. The powerful Wall showed no emotions. It was built to drive away the strong nomads. How could it but look down on her with contempt, a mere frail human being? She was faced with a brutal and hateful monster which had the passion for power but not for love and whose virtue consisted in absolute indifference to human misery. Completely beaten and exhausted, "she sat down and wept."

We can almost see with our mind's eye the solitary figure of Lady Meng in the walled-in wilderness, with tears running down her pale cheeks. We are no stranger to such tears. We have seen such tears of despair in mothers and fathers, in brothers and sisters, and in wives and husbands, when their loved ones were roused from sleep at night, seized at their work, taken away, held incommunicado for weeks and months, and sentenced to long prison terms. Their crime: speaking out for human rights and democracy. Here is a prayer a Korean mother said at a prayer meeting when her two sons were arrested:

> O God, since our beloved sons have been in prison, spring has passed, and summer has changed into chilly fall, and in a few days we will be celebrating *Ch'usok* (Harvest Moon Festival). We cannot keep back our tears. Since there is no way to still the sorrow of our hearts, at times we have wandered around on a lonely mountaintop crying aloud to you. And we have spent night-long prayer vigils putting our plea before you with tears. [10]

Are these not the tears of Lady Meng? Are these not our tears? How can this passionate plea with tears not move people? How can it fail to move God?

But the Wall is not moved. It has no tears. Nor is the ruling power moved. It too has no tears. This is hard to believe, but it is true. History is full of such "immovable" walls. The world has no lack of such "tear-less" ruling powers. In 1948 nearly a million poor Indian Tamils on Sri Lanka's tea plantations were suddenly deprived of their citizenship. They are descendants of the poverty-stricken landless workers brought over by the British landlords from South India more than a century ago to work the coffee plantations in the Kandy Highlands. For them Sri Lanka had become their home. But under agreements reached between the Indian and Sri Lankan governments many of them were to be repatriated to India. Here is an eyewitness report on a repatriation scene:

> There was much weeping and wailing. Some of the women were beating their breasts, knowing that they would never see their homeland again, the place where they were born, the countryside where they toiled, the home where they married, where they gave birth to their children, ate, drank, danced and slept, performed their religious ceremonies and buried their dead. Destined to see these familiar places no more, they were as if they were being torn apart, severed in two.[11]

The weeping, wailing and beating of the breasts must have been a mighty plea moving God's heart. The eyewitness was terribly moved. But the rulers who had made the repatriation agreements were not moved.

"Whose decision was this?" — this was the question in the minds and on the lips of those to be repatriated. Their question turned into a plea mixed with anger and helplessness. They poured their weeping and wailing into verses:

The rulers alone decided
That we leave this land
And go across the sea
And the loved one is separated
From the beloved.

Separated from the goats and cows
We reared so lovingly,
And the dog that followed us
So gratefully.

On the sea between Lanka and India
Separated lovers groan
And mourn of what will become
Of hearts long knit into one.

Others watch and sigh
As we from each other part
With unrestrained cries
And tears which flow.

The ties that bound us
To those with whom we worked
Are broken for ever
By our departure. ...

I do not know, O God
What is there in store for me;
Only let me have your grace
To live with your blessing.[12]

Tears bring together people in suffering. Through tears their hearts are united. But rulers seem to have an infinite ability to separate them, break their one heart, render them homeless.

But people can run out of tears. They are not tear-less like the Great Wall, like those who wield autocratic power. Of course not. They are, in fact, tear-*ful*. They have great capacity for tears. They feel, they love, they argue, they quarrel, and they weep. Tears are part of their life. Tears make them human, enabling them to be vulnerable to one another, to be available to one another, to be brothers and sisters in happiness and in misery. But the time may come when their tears run dry, their passion is extinguished, their love destroyed, and their zeal to live vanishes. That is the end of time, end of life — an apocalyptic time! Such a time has come to many people. A Vietnamese poet dedicated a poem to such an apocalyptic time of tearless-ness as the war around him raged on and on mercilessly:

I hammer the pain of separateness
into a statue to stand in the park.
Below it I carve a horizontal inscription
that reads: Soul of the Twentieth Century.

My statue sheds no tears
for it has none left to spend.
My statue tells no stories
for what's the use of telling stories?

My statue: the soul of the century
with no halos above its head.
My statue: the soul of the century
with no phoenixes beneath its feet.

My statue in fact is bare, naked,
no banner in its hand.
My statue casts its shadows aimless, everywhere,
with stone eyes fixed on Nothing.[13]

It must have been with excruciating pain that the poet wrote
this poem. How much he must have wished to be able to put
his poetic talent to the service of life filled with promise and
vitality, to sing in praise of noble humanity!

There is first of all the pain of separation — the pain that
separates the Tamils in Sri Lanka through repatriation, the
pain that separates the loved ones in the midst of senseless
war, and the pain that separates human beings from God.
Has separation — this cruel monster — become the soul of
the twentieth century? This is a horrible thought, but the
Vietnamese poet with his sensitive mind may be right. He
may not be indulging in poetic fantasy. Our world is
geopolitically separated. It is ideologically divided. Our
human community is racially torn. It is subject to social prejudices that distort human nature. Even Christians are still
separated at the Lord's Table on account of traditions,
canons and doctrines. And how our heart has lost the power
to resist the forces that separate us! It easily believes in
divisive gossip. It quickly yields to the temptation to achieve
one's own interest at the cost of others'.

The pain of separation will bring to an end the human
ability to tell stories. This is the next point the poet is making. His statue has no stories to tell. What a dreadful condi-
tion we human beings have created for ourselves! Our
history should be full of stories. In fact we have been telling
a number of stories. We have told stories in mythologies, in

legends, in folktales. We have recounted our life in poetry, in prose, in drama, and in dances. Around the supper table children, parents and grandparents sit, eat and tell stories. They tell funny stories, interesting stories and strange stories. They smile and laugh at these stories. Their hearts are united in that remarkable ability to tell stories, the ability to disclose themselves to one another. They also tell sad stories, painful stories and heart-rending stories. They sigh and shed tears for these stories. They long for a future community in which all hard-heartedness and atrocities will cease.

But the poet laments that there are no stories left to tell. History, for humankind in the twentieth century, has come to a stop. The world, in this technological age, has come to a standstill. Is there still history when there are no more stories to tell? Is there a human community when people have lost the ability to tell stories to one another? This is a dreadful thought, but it may be true. For you and I have seen those faces of children, men and women, strangely expressionless, hollow eyes staring into the void, and mouths without strength to complain or appeal. We have had a foretaste of an apocalyptic world without any stories left to tell.

The poet's verdict on this kind of world is that it is a statue without tears. "My statue sheds no tears," he says. His statue is no ordinary statue. It is a statue built with care and love. It is a statue inspired by a promise of life, and it pointed to the future of life. The poet calls it "the soul of the century." When this statue, this soul of the century, sheds no more tears, humanity faces a really big catastrophe. The world without tears is a heartless world. The soul that sheds no tears is a soul without love. What bigger catastrophe does humanity need for self-destruction?

O God, save us from turning into statues of tearless-ness! This must be our prayer. Tears are signs of life; they bring life back to the world. Tears well out of the heart of love; they restore to the human community the ability to love. Tears take form in cries and struggles for justice; they revive the soul of our century for a promise and a future. And it is in the people capable of tears that a promise of human community and a future for the world lie.

That is why people must not run out of tears. We must resist turning into statues of tearlessness at all cost. We must continue to be able to shed tears no matter what happens. We must save our tears and have them in plenty. We must have tears for public prayer meetings where we can pray in tears for political prisoners. There will be many occasions for us to mourn, with tears in our eyes, for injustice done to helpless people. In many of the societies to which we belong, it is time for public mourning. True, many of our repressive regimes want us to believe that this is a time of public festivity. Don't you see that our gross national product is up to 10% — so much better in comparison with five years ago? Don't you realize that our per capita income has risen this year to US $1,000 from US $950 last year? That is what they tell us. They point us to government statistics. So they do not like our tears. They are annoyed at our tear-ful prayer meetings. But, as long as there are political prisoners in our nation, every day is a day of public mourning. As long as prisoners of conscience are held in isolated camps, each day should not pass without the shedding of tears.

Our Jesus is a man of tears. He must have wept a lot. When he heard that Lazarus had died and been removed to a tomb, he wept (John 11:35). It is human to weep. And if we believe that Jesus is God incarnate, then it is also divine to weep. Those who saw Jesus weep for Lazarus said: "How dearly he must have loved him!" (John 11:36). Tears mean the capacity for love. Those who have no capacity for love have no tears. It is only when you love deeply, only if you love dearly, that you can weep. A stone has no capacity for love: it cannot weep. An autocratic power has no tears: it has no capacity for love. To maintain its power, it orders ten thousand lives to be extinguished without even blinking an eyelid. Tears are signs of humanity and divinity. Through our tears we may still keep this world human and divine.

Jesus must have had such thoughts in his mind when he argued heatedly with the religious authorities of his day. "Alas for you, lawyers and Pharisees, hypocrites!" — he was heard saying this over and over. He also boldly challenged the political authorities of the Roman colonialists. When Pilate the Roman governor tried to intimidate him with the formidable Roman authority, Jesus replied calmly: "You would have no authority at all over me if it had not been granted you from above" (John 19:11). Deep in his heart, Jesus must have been weeping. We are told that this same Jesus lamented over Jerusalem and said: "O Jerusalem, Jerusalem, the city that murders the prophets and stones the messengers sent to her! How often have I longed to gather your children, as a hen gathers her brood under her wings; but you would not let me" (Matthew 23:37; Luke 13:34). Jesus must have been in tears when these words burst from his lips. These are "words of lungs and intestines" *(fei-fu chi yen)* as one would put it in Chinese. These are sincere words — words that come from the heart, soul and body. The language we have here is the heart-language, soul-language, and body-language. It is the language on which you have staked your all. It is the language which embodies Jesus' capacity of love — for Lazarus, for friends, for the helpless and for the powerless. In this language of "lungs and intestines", Jesus has also shown his capacity of love even for the enemies and oppressors.

There was a towering figure who was capable of coming close to Jesus' language of "lungs and intestines". It was Gautama the Buddha. This is what was said about him:

> Because he saw them (humankind) living in an evil time, subjected to tyrannous kings and suffering many ills, yet heedlessly following after pleasure,
> For this he was moved to pity.
> Because he saw them living in a time of wars, killing and wounding one another: and knew that for the riotous hatred that has flourished in their hearts they were doomed to pay an endless retribution,
> For this he was moved to pity.[14]

"For this the Buddha was moved to pity." Pity is a deceptive word. It can be a misleading expression. It is perhaps more correct to say: "For this the Buddha was moved to tears." Why not? I am sure none of us has seen a Buddha face in painting or in sculpture with a trace of tears on it. Tears do not seem to fit in with our image of the Buddha.

He seems a personification of calmness itself. Seated in the lotus fashion, he is a model of oriental tranquillity. Nothing seems to disturb him. With his eyes half-closed, his ears closed to all worldly noises, he raises his hand ever ready to teach the other-worldly secrets of *nirvana*. But it is this very Buddha who is capable of being moved to tears. It is time we Christians gained the ability to look into the heart of the Buddha readily moved to tears in this turbulent sea of tyranny and war.

Jesus is moved to tears. The Buddha is moved to tears. What does this say? It says that people are moved to tears. It also says that God is moved to tears. Here we grasp a vital aspect of our political theology. Here we have the possibility of a power ethic. Our political theology is not a theocratic interpretation of structures of government as ordained by God. Both Luther and Calvin overplayed that kind of political theology, claiming St Paul as their mentor. Most western political theology has inherited this "orthodox" Reformation theology. As to our power ethic, it is not the ethic of the power that gives approval to violence in the theory and execution of revolution. Some of the Latin American political theology of liberation tempts us in this direction, with its acceptance of the Marxist analysis of class struggle as providing a scientific explanation of world history.

The source of our political theology in Asia is the people — the people humiliated, oppressed and impoverished. And the power of our political ethic comes from people's tears — tears people shed because of their misery and the misery of others. People capable of crying, people capable of being moved to weep — this is the source and power of our political theology. After all, did not Jesus weep for Jerusalem? Was he not moved to tears by the sick and by the outcasts? That is why we cannot think of the world without Jesus. In a much similar way we can also ask: After all, was not the Buddha moved to tears at the sight of "living multitudes" (*chung-sheng* in Chinese) in misery and suffering? That is why we cannot think of Asia without the Buddha.

Power of Tears

We have no illusions. We know politics is power. We have learnt our bitter lessons — in Korea, in Taiwan, in the Philippines, in Thailand, and even in India, the largest democracy in the world in terms of population. Power-politicians speak the language of power. They know no other language. They make people breathe it and eat it. They know people cannot and will not digest it. But no matter. The language of power must be the language of the land. Martial law or not, power-politicians see to it that people get the message in the language of power.

What then is the language of people's political theology? What must then be the semantics of people's power ethic? It is the language and the semantics created by people's tears. The language of tears versus the language of power! The power of tears against the power of guns! The outcome of the contest seems decided from the very beginning. The battle seems lost even before it begins.

But our folktale tells us an amazing story. Lady Meng's weeping "so affected the wall," we are told, "that it collapsed and laid bare her husband's bones!" Truly astonishing, the power of Lady Meng's tears! She must have wept her heart out. Her wailing must have moved the firmament of heaven and shaken the foundations of the earth. Her crying must have stirred all "living souls" (*sheng-ling* in Chinese) to rally behind her. And an incredible thing happened. The Wall, that invincible Wall, the Wall that embodied brutal power and naked authority, collapsed and yielded up her husband's bones!

Who says tears have no power? Who says only the weak shed tears? The tears that well out of the heart of love can cause the Great Wall to fall. Wan Sang Han, a Korean Christian layperson active in struggles for human rights and democracy, says this in a meditation entitled "In our Weakness is our Strength":

> We are weak. We are daily conscious of our weakness before the Leviathan of political power. ... However, our weakness and our powerlessness paradoxically operate as the basis of our strength. The powerful are keenly aware of our powerlessness and weakness, and at the same time afraid of it. Many of the policemen who follow us daily have confessed that they respect Christian conscientious objectors for their courage and weakness, even though they are constantly harassing us. It is indeed true that genuine courage comes from the weak.[15]

These words of Wan Sang Han are full of contradictions. He confesses that he and his comrades are weak and yet they are strong. This is a true confession. On the other hand, there are police agents, those who enforce martial law and order, who, though tremendously powerful, confess that they are afraid. This also is a true confession. What are we to make of such contradictions? Is it just a typical oriental habit of self-depreciation? Is this a commonplace trick we Asians are good at in our social conduct? When a host spreads before the astonished eyes of the guests a sumptuous twelve-course dinner, he or she says with barely concealed pride: "I am sorry there is not much to eat. But please help yourself!"

Christians and others involved in human rights efforts cannot afford the luxury of such verbal tricks. And functionaries of government security departments have no need of such hospitality acrobatics. What takes place is a straight confrontation of weakness with strength, powerlessness with power. It is an unequal contest between the weak and the strong. But in the thick of the battle, the weak realize that they are strong, while the strong confess that they are weak. Why? The strength of the weak is the strength of people's tears — tears that flow from the soul that longs for justice, from the heart that loves and cares. Who can withstand such power? Even the powerful Great Wall could not. How much less those secret service agents who keep close watch on victims of authoritarian power!

Love is stronger than might. People's tears are mightier than rulers' naked power. This is no sentimental platitude. This is, in fact, the heart of the Incarnation. "God loved the world so much," John tells us in his Gospel, "that God sent his Son into the world..." (3:16). God could have overpowered the world by a great might. People in the Old Testament often invoked a powerful God when they confronted their enemies. The Jews in Jesus' time expected a mighty God to come to their aid and shatter the Roman colonial power. We Christians too have inherited this tradition of worshipping a powerful and mighty God. We have associated with God the power to hurt, kill and destory. The God of the Exodus who let the Egyptian armies drown in the Red Sea and rescued the Hebrews from slavery has been a model-God for many Christians. But this model-God was not the God of Jesus Christ. This God "loved the world so much" that God chose to be present in Jesus and in what Jesus had to go through all the way from his birth in a manger to his death on the cross. This is a very unmodel-God. But it is this unmodel-God who keeps the world from breaking up into pieces and from falling into utter hopelessness.

We need only to recall the confession of the Roman soldier at the foot of Jesus' cross. That Roman soldier, completely armed from head to toe, is completely disarmed by Jesus on the cross armed with nothing but two pieces of wood, a symbol of shame, wretchedness and death. What moved him to confess that Jesus is the Son of God? Jesus' powerful tears! His undefeatable love! The soldier must have heard him pray to God: "Father, forgive them!" Jesus could not have said it in a loud voice, for he had already grown very weak. He could not have uttered it in a confident manner, for he was already on the verge of death. But there must have been great power in that feeble prayer. There must have been irresistible love supporting Jesus' weakened voice. That power of love won the heart of the Roman soldier.

Love has this strange power of turning the weak into the strong and the strong into the weak. It is because love is a moral power. The weak with such moral power become unafraid. It enables them to stand between heaven and earth conscious of being a part of the redemptive force at work in human community. In contrast, the strong, confronted with such moral power, lose their confidence in their power. They realize that the power they have is immoral power. And of course immoral power has no positive part to play in human history. The immoral power in their possession will eventually deny them a place in the march of history towards the future. How can they not become afraid when the future will be denied to them? The moral power of the weak is the crisis of the immoral power of the strong.

Love is also a spiritual power. Love is the power of the spirit against the power of the body. When the weak become conscious of the power of the spirit in command of the weak body, they can stand before those in power free and undeterred. The spirit-filled body is a strong body. Yes, that body can be arrested, put on trial and imprisoned. But bound, it is free; under trial, it bears witness to the best that God has given to humanity; imprisoned, it discovers the space and time of hope that conquers the space and time of despair.

Here is a poem written by a Taiwanese pastor serving a six-year prison sentence for having been involved in human rights activities. The prison is located in a place called the Tortoise Mountain in northern Taiwan.

I am a passenger
on a train of life going forward.
Mr Driver:
At this station, the Tortoise Mountain,
Please stop for a while!
Not to stay here for ever,
but — just for a while!
Please wait until I have gained
some precious experiences of life.

Though the price is rather high,
Yet, can "precious things" be purchased at a bargain?
Can life's experience be gained easily?
Here, I see many many stars,
I have also seen clouds in the blue sky.
I cannot buy stars, nor can I reach the clouds.
I wait quietly for the cheerful news from the sun,
and fill it in a basket to the brim.
So,
I am going to stop at this station, the Tortoise Mountain,
For a while![16]

There is no fretting in this poem, for a spirit-filled body
does not fret. Nor is there any outburst of hate in it, for a
body filled with the spirit is incapable of hate; it is only
capable of love.

What kind of power then is the power of love? It is a
divine power. "God so loved the world..." That is why
there is love in the world. That is why love is possible in the
human community. That is why love remains the power
that can turn history upside down. And that is why the
authoritarian power that hates, imprisons, kills and
destroys, is not the last word for humanity. At most it is a
word before the last. It is a word which has no finality. It is
not an ultimate word. The final and ultimate word belongs
to love. That is God's word. Jesus Christ is this word of
God. No wonder he is strong, though he is weak; he is
powerful, though he is powerless; he is filled with truth,
though he falls a victim to lies. Do we still have any doubt as
to why love is the heart of Jesus' political theology? Can we
still question why Jesus has made love the secret of his
power ethic?

Encounter with Truth
The Great Wall collapsed, and Lady Meng retrieved her
husband's bones. The struggle seems over and her heart's
desire won. We could wish her godspeed as she set out on
her return journey with the precious memory of her husband. But an uneventful home-bound trek it was not going
to be. A greater ordeal was still to come. The emperor had

heard about her and wanted to see her. When she was brought to him, her beauty so struck him that he wanted to make her empress! Anger is the only fitting reaction to the emperor's outrageous design. Do you remember the prophet Nathan who became fiercely angry when King David had Uriah killed on the battlefield and took Bathsheba, Uriah's wife, and made her queen (2 Sam. 12:1-14)?

But besides anger, a deep theology on authoritarian power is hidden in this Chinese folktale. The folktale wants to tell us that autocratic power is the power that rapes. It rapes people's conscience. It rapes people's beauty. It rapes people's virtue. This is the power behind the Great Wall. This is the power that proclaims martial law. This is the power that promulgates a new constitution in the name of a sham democracy.

Lady Meng is brought face to face with this power that rapes. What could she do? What could people do? Submit to it? Yes, people have submitted unwillingly to the power that oppresses them, impoverishes them and humiliates them. Rebel against it? Yes, people have risked their lives and rebelled. The Chinese saying, rulers compel people to rebel, is an apt description of it both in a feudal society in the past and in an authoritarian nation today. In many

50

instances, it is secret societies and religious groups which
head rebellions.

Launch a revolution? Yes the history of each nation is a
history of revolutions. One tyrannous dynasty is replaced by
another tyrannous dynasty through revolution. In the
modern history of Asian nations, revolution has often
turned out military regimes and police states.

Lady Meng did not rebel. Nor did she start a revolution.
But was there anything left for her to do if she neither
rebelled nor rose up in revolution? All she could have done,
it would seem, was to resign to her fate and submit to the
emperor's brutal passion. She would have had to "swallow
all her tears into her stomach," as a Chinese saying goes.
For countless men and women in China and, for that matter, in the world, throughout history, "swallowing tears into the stomach" has been the only choice under an oppressive situation. A daughter-in-law in a traditional
Chinese family had to swallow her tears into her stomach
under the domination of a severe and fault-finding mother-
in-law. Children had to swallow their tears into their
stomachs before an authoritarian father. But above all it is
an autocratic ruler who forces his subjects to swallow their
tears into their stomachs.

The stomachs of people under an autocratic ruler are
filled with bitter tears. They cry within them. They groan in-
side their bodies. They shout and protest in the secret of
their hearts, but murmur compliments and put on smiles
before their authoritarian ruler. People are drowned in their
own bitter tears and suffocated with their own silent cries.
But those in power do not see the tears, do not hear the
cries, and have no feeling for people's agony in body and in
spirit.

Lady Meng's stomach must have been bursting with her
bitter tears. But what could she do? Submit to the emperor?
If she did not rebel and start a revolution, she did not submit either. She turned the encounter with the power that
rapes into an encounter with the truth! To face the brutal
power with no dagger or spear but only with the truth —
surely this takes more courage than organizing an armed
rebellion. To stand in front of the cruel ruler, defended not

by a matching power but only by the naked truth — surely this involves a risk far greater than an organised revolution. But this is what Lady Meng did.

She had the emperor construct a terrace forty-nine feet high on the bank of the river in preparation for her husband's burial. She requested that the emperor and all his officials be present on the occasion. What a picture the folkstory teller paints before our eyes! Standing there on the

terrace forty-nine feet high is a single frail woman consumed with love for her dead husband and with truth about the inhumanity of the ruling power. Down below is the whole empire of the ruthless power that thrives on exploiting the helpless and powerless people. The contrast between beauty and ugliness, humanity and inhumanity, truth and lie, love and hate, is so great that it appears grotesque. People's tears and the rulers' power confront each other for a showdown. The invisible tension between the two parties must have been so tense that it could snap at any moment.

The tension did snap. In the full view of the emperor and all his officials present, Lady Meng "began to curse the emperor in a loud voice for all his cruelty and wickedness." She poured out her tears in a torrent of truth about the empire of the cruel power. She forced the powers that be to see her tears, to hear her cries and to face her agonies. She compelled the inhuman ruling power to face for the first time the noble humanity in this humiliated woman, in the oppressed people, and in the victims of brutality.

This is the moment of encounter with truth. The emperor must have shaken in fury. His officials must have trembled with fear. Everybody says the emperor is virtuous and wise. Court officials say so. People so acclaim him. Inscriptions on numerous stone monuments erected on sacred mountains so proclaim. One of these stone monuments reads:

> The sage emperor who has pacified all under heaven is
> tireless in his rule;
> He rises early, goes to sleep late, makes lasting
> benefits and offers wise instructions;
> Wide spread his teachings, all far and near is well ordered
> according to his will. ...[17]

The words sound so familiar, don't they? They might have come straight out of many government-controlled newspapers in many countries in today's Asia. All praise to presidents and party chairmen! Another stone monument sums it all up in these words:

> His (the emperor's) achievements surpass those of the
> Five Emperors;
> His kindness reaches even the beasts of the field;
> All creatures benefit from his virtue,
> All live in peace at home.[18]

Paradise has dawned under the rule of Shih Huang-ti!

All this is an absolute lie of course. What we have in an autocratic state is an autocracy by white lies. It is a magic power that an autocratic ruler has. He can turn his lies into truths and people's truths into lies. It is formidable, this magic power. The ruling machinery, from top to bottom, is run totally by this magic power. All the way from the martial law court judge to the prison guard that magic power spares no one. They mouth the lies of their ruler as if they are divine oracles from heaven and condemn people's truth as if they are blasphemies against the state authorities. Lies provide a kind of self-intoxication for the ruler on the one hand, and on the other they serve to lock the people in a captivity of the heart, mind and soul.

Lies are an indispensable part of power politics. Lies and power join forces to crush any slightest disclosure of truth. And the sad fact is that political and economic forces in the West join hands with power politicians in the Third World for the suppression of truths and the promotion of lies. In Asia, for example, a story like the following illustrates the situation of complicity which the power of lies has created:

> Throughout Asia, the gap between the rich and the poor is widening. In countries like the Philippines, Korea, Malaysia, Sri Lanka and Taiwan, free trade zones have been established to attract foreign corporations, with large pools of cheap labour, flexible labour laws and tax exemptions. The result has been disastrous on the peasant class who have moved from the farms to these zones in the hope of getting much-needed jobs and financial stability. Instead they have often become virtual slaves in these zones, living in serious poverty and with little protection from their government while the foreign corporations and the ruling elite rake in vast amounts of profits.[19]

Those who hold political and economic power stamp out such truths as lies, of course. According to them people are happy, prosperous and contented. A new era of economic industry has begun, and people enjoy freedom and democracy. How long are we to submit to such lies disguised as truths? How much longer is it possible for the world, both East and West, to make profit out of rejecting people's truths as lies?

But on that terrace on the river bank Lady Meng ceases to be a prisoner of lies. She is in full command of truth now. In the entire hearing of those manufacturers of lies, she lets the truth out. "You, the emperor, are wicked and brutal!" she shouted. For the first time the emperor and his officials encountered truth. At that moment Lady Meng commands the empire of truth and defeats the empire of lies.

People have the truth. This is an audacious thing to say, I know. It can be a dangerous assertion to make. We must not make such truth-claim about everything; otherwise we, each one of us, become little dictators dictating truth itself and dictating others to think, know and believe as we do.

That is where religious intolerance comes in. That is where obscurantism prevails. People can err, of course. As a matter of fact, they have often erred. We remember the story of the golden calf in the Old Testament. In the absence of Moses, they persuaded Aaron, the acting leader, into "making gods to go ahead of them" (Exodus 32). People can be manipulated to serve the particular interests of certain power groups. This is the case with the crowds who welcome Jesus into Jerusalem shouting hosannas but demand his death shortly afterwards. Still fresh in our memory are the millions of Red Guards running through the length and breadth of China, with the little red book in their hands, at the behest of their charismatic leader. No, we must not make idols of people. People are no gods. We must remember this in our theology of people.

There are situations, however, in which people have the truth — situations in which people are oppressed, condemned to poverty and deprived of freedom of conscience. When Lady Meng, whose husband was murdered for the building of the Wall, says that the emperor is cruel and wicked, the emperor must indeed be cruel and wicked. When Australian aborigines lament that "until our land rights are recognized, we cannot be free and equal citizens with white Australians'',[20] white Australians must indeed be treating them as unfree and unequal citizens. When the majority of the people in Taiwan protest that they have no political rights of self-determination, the ruling regime must indeed be depriving them of their political rights of self-determination. If the poor in the slums and shanties of the big cities of Asia complain that they suffer exploitation at the hands of giant industries and multinational corporations, these industries and multinational corporations must indeed be exploiting them. In this sense, people have the truth; and the truth must be said and heard.

Encounter with truth is the heart of our political theology. The politics of love does not have to lead to the politics of vengeance and the politics of violence. But it must lead to the politics of truth. The prophets in the Old Testament played the politics of truth to the hilt. It was the only politics they knew. To Shallum, King of Judah, the prophet Jeremiah declared:

But you have no eyes, no thought for anything but gain,
set only on the innocent blood you can shed,
on cruel acts of tyranny (Jeremiah 22:17).

The king has no eyes. He is blinded by lies. He must be brought face to face with truth — the truth of the people who suffer under his tyranny.

In Jesus, the politics of truth becomes an ultimate politics. "I am the truth," he said (John 14:6). Jesus is the truth that the sabbath is made for people and not people for the sabbath. He is the truth that the poor who suffer now will fare better in the reign of God than the rich insensitive to the misery of the poor. He is the truth that the hungry have the human right to rice and the well-fed have the human duty to share with them their abundant rice. He is also the truth that the oppressed people are entitled to the day when they can "raise their heads above the sky", while oppressors have the moral obligation to yield their power to the people through unrigged elections.

I do not think that Jesus was idolizing poverty in the place of wealth, or commending the hungry at the expense of the well-fed. Nor do I believe that he was encouraging sighing and weeping, or ridiculing merry-making and rejoicing.

Jesus did not indulge in "sour-grape" theology. He was a poor carpenter, to begin with. That is true. But he was almost crowned as king. Power and wealth were within his reach. These were his for the asking. In this regard, the story of the temptation shows a most human side of Jesus. Power, glory and riches! Who would not be tempted by them? Even Jesus was! But he rejected them. Why? In Jesus' ultimate political ethic, truth cannot avoid conflict with the ruling power. How true this is in the case of an authoritarian regime! But it can also be true with a democratic government. In Jesus' ultimate power ethic, truth is a difficult companion of wealth. How true this is in a capitalist society! But it can also be true in a socialist society. Jesus' politics is truth-politics; his power ethic is love ethic. And it is on the basis of his truth politics and love ethic that Jesus wants us to re-adjust radically our concept of justice and design our strategy for securing it.

We may at once recall Jesus' parable of the labourers in the vineyard (Matthew 20:1-5). The labourers in the parable were hired at five different times on the same day — early morning, midmorning, midday, mid-afternoon, and an hour before sunset. When the day ended and payment was made, the labourers discovered that they all received the same wages, from those who laboured ten hours to those who worked only for one hour. Obviously, this was a grave injustice. But Jesus saw it differently. Justice, in Jesus' view, consists in everyone each day having enough to live on. We can be sure that in his parable the wages represented this adequate sum. This is the truth involved in the landowner's wage politics. But there was something more. The wages were given with love. The labourers who complained bitterly could not, of course, understand this. They did not realize that justice, blind to the needs of others and divorced from love for others, is no justice at all. It is tyranny. It is inhumanity. This is jungle politics and jungle ethics — survival of the fittest. But the heart of Jesus' political theology and his power ethic is just the opposite — survival of the unfittest. That is why his God has a determined bias for the prodigal son. That is why Jesus sides with prostitutes, tax-collectors and the poor. He seeks out a particular kind of people, the unfittest people, re-instates them in society and gives them a prominent place in the reign of God. You may call Jesus' vision of the future human community that of "from each according to his or her ability, to each according to his or her need." So be it! The fundamental driving force behind Jesus' vision is truth and love, and not lie and violence.

Many people in Asia, Christians and others, are becoming more and more engaged in the mission of encounter with truth in the service of the vision of human community in which the unfittest become the fittest.Truth must be spoken out loud. We want to saturate ruling powers with the truth of suffering people. We want to inundate those in high authorities with the true state of the people in despair. Senator Jovito R. Salonga, for example, tells us what it is really like in the Philippines:

70% of the population are malnourished;

85% of school children suffer from protein-calorie malnutrition;

70% of Manila residents today are poor, and 40% are very poor.[21]

This is people statistics. And there are ample reasons to believe that this people statistics is much more true than government statistics. In every nation Christians and others must let such people statistics shout and cry in the ears of the authorities until they can no longer stand it.

In the 1980 Christmas issue of *Taiwan Church News* appeared a short article, "Let's Talk Again: The President too is a Human Being":

> ... President too is a human being, thus his words are not sacred oracle. His instruction is not heavenly truths which people must obey. The President is not an emperor. In a democratic society the President is the people's public servant. The difference between a public servant and an emperor is like the difference between heaven and abyss.... President too is a human being. We should respect him, but not worship him. We should accept him with reasons, and not praise him blindly.[22]

This is people's logic. It should be the political logic in a nation that professes to be free and democratic. But in

58

certain self-styled democratic countries in Asia, presidents have their own political logic: it is for them to dictate and rule, and it is for people to listen and obey. This kind of self-styled democracy will not do. It must be said loud and clear that the presidents' logic is false and that the people's logic is true. We must, with the people's logic, argue and reason until rulers cannot ignore it.

This kind of people's statistics and people's logic is now beginning to appear in abundance in Asia. It does not have national or ideological boundaries. Let me quote a Peking underground poem called *Today*:

What did Cain come to the world for?
— to turn light into darkness,
— to turn joy into pain,
— to turn love into tragedy.
O Poet, please strip away his mask;
Then,
All pain and groanings
like drops of water will gather together
raising giant waves that level the mountains and empty the sea.
Each and every obscure thought
will become crystallized like atomic energy
releasing enormous power to destroy everything.
At that time, people
will no longer be a powerless hand
forced to raise in unconditional acceptance
of the dictator's order. ...[23]

This is peoples's song. How authentic it sounds! It sounds authentic because it comes out of people's heart — a heart harassed, wounded, oppressed, a heart seeking to be free, to be human and to be open. Party leaders' songs, in contrast, are political rhetoric without human authenticity. These songs praise the greatness of the party, the government, and its policies. They extol the virtues and achievements of its leaders. They intimidate the people into conformity and build walls around people's hearts.

But the wounded heart of the people must sing. It must ask why Cain came into the world "to turn light into darkness, to turn joy into pain, to turn love into tragedy."

These are the questions people ask behind closed doors, whisper in each other's ears, and turn over and over in their hearts during sleepless nights.

But people do not just ask questions. They also hope. They long for the day when "all pain and groanings will gather together, raising giant waves that level the mountains and empty the sea." This is the great vision of that great unknown prophet known as Second Isaiah among the Jews in exile in Babylon. This ancient vision has turned out to be not ancient at all. It is a modern vision, a vision so contemporary and so timely. Nor is it a vision only a great prophet such as Second Isaiah is capable of. The author of the poem *Today* proves that ordinary men and women, especially those under oppresive situations, are also capable of such a vision.

As long as there is still such a vision among the people, there is hope for a society, for a nation, and for the world. Such vision must be kept alive, cultivated and developed until it becomes a reality some day. For the advent of that day such underground people's songs as *Today* must be sung again and again until they become an above-ground song. To that day the unknown poet in Peking must have dedicated this poem and this song.

A Grand Finale

It is a passionate political theology we have in the folktale "The Faithful Lady Meng." It shows us a paradoxical power ethic too — a power ethic not built on powerfulness but on powerlessness. This is a deeply inspiring political theology and power ethic. But the critical point to remember is that powerlessness can transform into powerfulness through the power of tears, that is, the power of love and truth. And the reverse can also be true. Powerfulness, when confronted by the power of tears, that is, the power of love and truth, can turn into powerlessness. It must be with such a conviction that our folkstory teller has taken us to an encounter with truth before the emperor and his court. But the story does not come to an end with such an encounter. With what can only be called deep theological insight our folkstory teller weaves the encounter with truth into an encounter with death and resurrection. And the drama we see here is as sublime as it is tragic, as Christian as it is Asian.

Encounter with truth is an encounter with death. "The truth will set you free" (John 8:32), says Jesus. This is true. But what kind of freedom is Jesus talking about here? Freedom from religious prejudices? Yes, Jesus had a lot to say about that. He deplored the religious prejudices that had developed among the Jews towards those outside their immediate community like the Samaritans. He told them the parable of the Good Samaritan to set them free from their religious prejudices. In many ways the faith of the religious leaders in Jesus' days was an arrogant faith. It had no room for persons conscious of their sins and weaknesses. Jesus told them a story about a Pharisee and a tax-collector who prayed in the temple and said that it was the tax-collector, not the Pharisee, who went home forgiven (Lk. 18:9-14). Jesus tried hard to set religious authorities free from their arrogance by driving home the truth that God favours a truly repentant heart and not an arrogant faith.

Yes, the truth sets Jesus free for God's business in the world. And it also sets many many people free from their pain, sorrow and fear. The poor, the hungry and the outcasts came to him seeking freedom from the shackles of life and the grip of fate. Jesus opened their eyes to the beauty of God's nature. He opened their mind to the inner quality of life. Above all, he opened their hearts to the God who loves them, worries with them, suffers with them. He brought God very,very close to people. In fact he is God to them, for God is in him and with him. When people see Jesus,they see God. When they hear him, they hear God. When they touch him, they touch God.

But the truth that sets powerless people free from their powerlessness does not set the powerful free from their power. That truth is a threat to them. Jesus the truth is a challenge to them. And the God who is so close to the people is dangerous to those in power. That truth is so threatening and dangerous that it must be put away. That is why, although Jesus the truth will set you free, enemies of the truth will not set you free. How can they set you free when they refused to set even Jesus the truth free from the cross and death?

Lady Meng must have known that. She climbed the steps of the terrace with truth on her lips and with death before her. After shouting the truth into the emperor's ears from the terrace she jumped into the river and embraced death. For her, encounter with truth becomes encounter with death.

The shadow of death is never far from truth. This is a sobering thought. Torture chambers are there to process truth into false confessions. Trials are staged to turn truth into lies. Prisons are built to keep truth out of the reach of the public. And killings are carried out to silence truth. Authoritarian power has this formidable weapon to deal with truth — death. We witness this today as Christians and others in Asia and elsewhere are submitted to torture, trial, imprisonment and even death for siding with truth.

This is a crime against truth. It is one of the oldest and most widespread crimes in the human community. And it is perhaps the most serious crime in our world today. Listen to this:

> There is no doubt that the practice of torture has been on the increase in recent years. There is no doubt that its use has been more widespread. There is no doubt that it is practised with the direct or implied permission of a large number of governments, many of whom consider themselves civilized. There is no doubt that, like a contageous disease, it spreads from one country to another, and, in many cases, is deliberately imported by the armed services of one country and taught to the services of another country.[24]

The powers which conquer, dominate and exploit, cannot stand the truth. The truth that the rich become richer and the poor become poorer, that the human spirit cannot be for ever chained to domination and dictatorship, is so *naked* that it must be covered with torture. That truth is so true that it must be guarded by the police force. That truth is so eloquent that it must be put to silence. This organized crime against truth defiles humanity, mocks people's tears, and defies the power of God's love.

There is of course nothing strange in this for Christians. The trial of Jesus before Pontius Pilate comes at once to our mind. To Pilate, bearer of Roman power and authority, Jesus said: "My task is to bear witness to the truth. For this was I born; for this I came into the world, and all who are not deaf to truth listen to my voice" (John 18:38-38).

Truth is a big word. It stands there right in front of us. But those blinded by their power cannot see it. Truth is a loud voice. But those deafened by the authority surrounding them cannot hear it. Truth is such an important fact of life. But those preoccupied with their own self-importance built on power and authority hardly appreciate its importance.

But Pilate at least saw it. For that very truth, Jesus, is there right in front of him. In fact he could not help seeing it because it was brought to his court to be tried by him. Pilate also heard it. For he had repeatedly demanded that truth to speak out for itself and was annoyed that it was silent. But now that it had spoken, he could not but hear it.

Pilate must have realized that it was an important truth with which he was confronted. For he asked: "What is truth?" At least he asked the right question, but he had no answer. He could not understand the truth that is Jesus. He could not see Jesus as the truth. The truth he understood is the truth of Roman power. The truth he saw is the truth of Roman authority. That is why he actually threatened Jesus with it. "I have authority to release you, and I have authority to crucify you" (John 19:10), he reminded Jesus. He did carry out his death threat and let Jesus the truth be crucified on the cross.

The cross could have been the end of it all. It did seem to be the end to many people. It seemed so to Jesus' own disciples. It also does seem that way to many of us. The cross closes the future for the oppressed people. It brings despair to the hungry. It adds sorrow to this already grim and sad world. If the cross on which Jesus was crucified is such a cross, let us forget it altogether. People should stop shedding tears and relying on the power of love. There must be other ways in which we could quickly bring about the fall of brutal emperors and hateful rulers.

But the cross of Jesus is *not* the end of it. This we all know. A tremendous power is released from it to defeat the power of death with the power of resurrection. Is it not because of this that the Roman soldier at the foot of Jesus' cross, as we have seen, confessed that Jesus was the Son of God? Is it not because of this that Jesus' disciples came out

of their hiding to bear witness to the very cross from which they had fled? And is it not because of this that the cross has never ceased to be the testimony to God's hope and future for humanity? Since this is the case, how is it possible for us as Christians not to let the power of life released from the cross inspire our political theology and create our power ethic?

Most surprisingly, our folktale seems not unaware of this kind of political theology and this kind of power ethic. When Lady Meng jumped to her death from the terrace, the emperor "flew into a rage and ordered his soldiers to cut up her body into little pieces and to grind her bones to powder." It was such a cruel power that Lady Meng had to face even in death. What the emperor did was to carry out an extreme form of revenge one could wreak on one's enemy in ancient China. The idea perhaps was to erase every trace of one's hated enemy from the face of the earth. Lady Meng's tears made the Great Wall crumble, but they did not break the emperor's heart. The emperor was determined to wipe out every bit of the truth she had disclosed in the hearing of the world. Her death, like the cross, seemed a most wasteful and futile thing. It only added to the cruelty and insanity of the emperor. Through death she escaped the fate

of rape. Perhaps that was only a personal triumph; her death seemed to have changed nothing at all as far as the oppressive power of the emperor was concerned.

But see how our folkstory teller transforms this revenge, with the horrible death which it brings, into the power of life that lives for ever! "As the emperor's soldiers did this," so the folktale brings us to its grand finale, "the little pieces of Lady Meng's body changed into little silver fish, in which the soul of the faithful Meng Chiang lives for ever." Here we touch the theological genius of our folktale. Death is not the end! The power of the emperor, brutal, cruel and inhuman as it is, is not the final power! Do we not catch in this an echo of what Jesus once said: "...a grain of wheat reamins a solitary grain unless it falls into the ground and dies; but if it dies, it bears a rich harvest" (John 12:24)?

Just imagine each little piece of Lady Meng's body, ground to powder, now turned into little living fish! There must have been hundreds, thousands, and even millions of them! And imagine again these countless fish, carrying the soul of Lady Meng in them, continuing to shed tears for the injustice done to them, to face authoritarian rulers with the power of love, and to speak the truth in public! Without such little fish, could there be a revolution to change the structures of injustice? Without such small citizens, would it be possible for democratic forces to confront autocratic forces? And without those helpless men and women armed only with the soul of Lady Meng, where could one find the human spiritual power to dream the dream of a just society, to plan for a future human community with peace, and to work towards a new creation promised to us by God?

The history of a nation does not consist mainly of emperors, kings or presidents. Nor is history primarily the history of revolutionary heroes. What makes history history are the people in whom the soul of Lady Meng lives — people humiliated and exploited, but awakened to challenge the power of death with the power of resurrection. People make history worth experimenting with and worth living. There is no failure in the history created by people. People's history never fails. What we read and see is the failure of the history of kings, emperors and dictators. But the people bear their history in pain. They carry it forward in suffering, and they create it in anticipation of its fulfilment. Is this not the history of the cross?

It is into this movement of people's history that we as Christians in Asia have become incorporated. We are not writing a "Christian" history of Asia. As long as we are intent on such a history, it becomes a missionary history, a history of confessions and denominations. But as we begin to write history with our fellow Asians, it turns out, to our surprise, to be a history of the cross and resurrection in Asia. The space created by the spiritual power of the cross and the resurrection expands progressively through the little silver fish in which the soul of Lady Meng lives. Our political theology is located in the spaces created by the spiritual power of Asian people in suffering. And our power ethic is the ethic that believes in the ultimate victory of God who lives with people and gives them the power of truth, love and justice. If this is God's politics, it should be ours also.

NOTES

[1] See *Folktales of China*, edited by Wolfram Eberhard (Chicago: The University of Chicago Press, 1965), pp. 25-26.

[2] See Kenneth Latourette, *The Chinese, their History and Culture* (New York: The Macmillan Company, 1959), p. 613.

[3] Peter L. Berger, *Pyramids of Sacrifice*, Political Ethics and Social Change (New York: Basic Books, Inc., 1974), p. 137.

[4] Herb Feith, "Repressive-Developmentalist Regimes in Asia: Old Struggles, New Vulnerabilities," in *Escape from Domination* (Tokyo: International Affairs—Christian Conference of Asia, 1979, pp. 49-73), p. 58.

[5] See "Human Sacrifice" in *Encyclopedia of Religion and Ethics*, ed. James Hastings (Edinburgh: T. & T. Clark, 1913), vol. VI, pp. 840-867.

[6] *Ibid.*, p. 840b.

[7] Quoted in J. A. Viera Gallo, "Arms Race in the Third World", in *The Security Trap*, a Concern for Christians, ed. José-Antonio Viera Gallo (Rome: IDOC International, 1979, pp. 50-59), p.51.

[8] See *International Herald Tribune*, February 20, 1981, p. 1.

[9] "U.S. Foreign Aid", an editorial in *International Herald Tribune*, January 30, 1981.

[10] From "A Mother's Prayer", in *Documents on the Struggle for Democracy in Korea*, ed. The Emergency Christian Conference on Korean Problems (Tokyo: Shinkyo Shuppansha, 1975), p. 205.

[11] *No Place in the Inn*, Voices of Minority Peoples in Asia (Urban Rural Mission — Christian Conference of Asia, 1979), p. 48.

[12] *Ibid.*, p. 49.

[13] Tru Vu, "The Statue of the Century", in *A Thousand Years of Vietnamese Poetry*, trans. Nguyen Ngoc Bich with Burton Raffel and W. S. Merwin (New York: Alfred A. Knopf, 1975), p. 179.

[14] See *The Wisdom of Buddhism*, ed. Christmas Humphreys (London: Curzon Press Ltd., 1979), p. 37.

[15] In *Varieties of Witness*, ed. D. Preman Niles & T.K. Thomas (Singapore: Christian Conference of Asia, 1980), p. 129.

[16] By Hsu Tien-Hsien, *Taiwan Church News*, April 26, 1981, p. 8 (translation from the Chinese by CSS).

[17] See Szuma Chien, *Records of the Historian*, trans. Yang Hsien-yi & Gladys Yang (Hong Kong: The Commercial Press, 1974), p. 169.

[18] *Ibid.*, p. 172. These legendary emperors in pre-historic China are, by one account, Huang-ti (Yellow Emperor), Chuan Hsiu, K'u, Yao, and Shun. They are revered as sage rulers.

[19] *Struggling with People is Living in Christ* (Urban Rural Mission — Christian Conference of Asia, 1981), p. 124.

[20] See *No Place in the Inn*, p. 15.

[21] See Salonga, "Seven Years of Martial Law in the Philippines, an Evaluation," in *Escape from Domination, op. cit.,* p. 76.

[22] *Taiwan Church News (Kau-Hoe Kong-Po)*, December 21 & 28, 1980, p. 7 (translation from the Chinese by CSS).

[23] From *Peking Spring*, a collection of poems and essays by Wei Ching-sheng & others (Peking: P'ing Ming Publishing House, 1980), pp. 352-3 (translation from the Chinese by CSS).

[24] In the opening address by Sean Macbride, SC, the Chairperson of the International Executive Committee of Amnesty's first International Conference on the Abolition of Torture, Paris, December 1973. See James Avery Joyce, *The New Politics of Human Rights* (London: The Macmillan Press Ltd., 1978), p. 83.